FUNSkills

Official Cambridge Exam Preparation

Home Booklet 4

David Valente

Reading

Read and choose the correct words and write them on the lines.

parrot

balcony

~~jungle~~

city centre

roller skates

milkshake

village

shopping centre

This is a rainforest with many trees, birds and monkeys.
Example
jungle

You can see this red, orange, yellow and blue bird in the rainforest.
1 _____

You can sit or stand here. It is a platform outside a house or flat.
2 _____

This is a cold, sweet drink with chocolate or fruit that you have in a café.
3 _____

You can find many buildings, bus stations, car parks, cinemas and a big square here.
4 _____

This is a small town, often in the countryside.
5 _____

Fun boost

Find a photo or draw a picture of your favourite place in your village, town or city.

Put your picture here

Where is it?
_____

What can you do there?
_____

Answer the three questions.

Why do you like it?
_____

Reading

Read the text and choose the best answer.

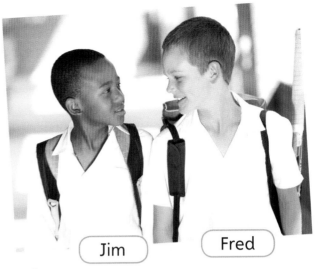

Jim   Fred

Example

Fred: How was your weekend?

Jim: (A:) It was brilliant. I saw someone famous at the shopping centre!

B: I'll ask my aunt and uncle.

C: My bedroom is very cold.

1

Jim: Where did you go on Saturday afternoon, Fred?

Fred: A: At three o'clock.

B: I'm staying home all afternoon.

C: I went to the swimming pool.

2

Fred: Did you go sailing with your family on Sunday morning, Jim?

Jim: A: I really love the sea.

B: We had a great time at the beach!

C: No, I didn't. I was sick.

3

Jim: What did you eat at the funfair on Friday evening?

Fred: A: My favourite food is meatballs and chips.

B: I had noodles and fish and a banana milkshake.

C: My dad can cook a cheese and tomato pizza.

4

Fred: What did you see from the top of the mountain on Saturday?

Jim: A: I saw the big waterfall in the forest.

B: I was really brave because it was dangerous.

C: I put on my big boots, a jacket and a helmet.

5

Jim: How much homework did you do at the weekend?

Fred: A: I asked the teacher.

B: I didn't do any. I'm really naughty!

C: I can play an exciting computer game.

Fun boost

Choose three of the Fun Skills characters. Tell your family EXCITING things about them. What did they do last weekend?

Reading

Read and choose the correct words and write them on the lines.

Sasha

present

temperature

point

●●● Sasha's blog

Don't feed the animals!

On Thursday, I went on a school trip to the zoo with my friends and Mrs Petrov, my English *teacher* . It was exciting to walk around and see all the different animals. We saw dolphins swimming in the pool and kangaroos jumping up and down on the grass.

The giant **1** _____ looked thirsty and hot under the tree because it was a really sunny day with a **2** _____ of about 30°. I **3** _____ my water bottle to give them a drink, but Mrs Petrov said, 'No, don't! It's too dangerous. They could bite your hand!'

Then we went to see the birds. They were many different colours. My favourite ones were the **4** _____. One was called Peter. He came and sat on my shoulder and asked, 'Sasha, how are you today?' It was VERY funny. My friends and I **5** _____ a lot. We had a brilliant day!

laughed

~~teacher~~

pandas

doctor

opened

parrots

Fun boost

Draw a comic about a trip to the bottom of the sea. Tell the story to your family.

1   What did you take?
2   How did you get there?
3   Who did you go with?
4   What fun things did you do?

Reading

Read and choose the correct words. Write them in the story.

All about sharks

Sharks are big fish that live **in** seas, rivers and lakes around the world. Some sharks live **1** _____ the beach and some live in the open sea. There are more than 500 shark families in the world. Some are smaller **2** _____ a person's hand, but the great white shark is the **3** _____ – more than six metres long!

Many sharks have long noses with very big mouths and heads. Most sharks **4** _____ small fish and have hundreds of teeth. Many people are afraid **5** _____ sharks, but sharks like to eat other fish, not people!

Example

A	in	B	on	C	at

....

1	A down	B near	C inside
2	A because	B when	C than
3	A biggest	B big	C bigger
4	A ate	B eaten	C eat
5	A off	B of	C out of

Fun boost

Make a Sea Animals Question Wheel. Ask and answer questions with your family.

1 Draw a circle and make 12 sections. Draw six animals – dolphin, shark, whale, crocodile, jellyfish, octopus – and write six questions: *What does it eat? Where does it live? What does it look like? Does it play? Can it talk? Do you like it?*

2 Draw another circle. Cut out two windows the same size as the sections and add the title: SEA ANIMALS QUESTION WHEEL.

3 Put the two circles together with a paper fastener. Turn the top wheel to play the game.

Reading

Look at the pictures and read the story. Draw and colour the six missing things.

Our island holiday

Last year, I went on a fantastic holiday to a beautiful island with my family. One day, Mum said my sister Eva and I could go sailing. Mum's boat was near ours, but Eva and I were excited to have a boat just for us.

The sun was in the sky and there were birds near our boat. It was great fun! We had some yummy sandwiches for lunch. Eva had an egg and tomato sandwich and I had a cheese sandwich.

When I opened my lunch bag, the boat moved quickly, my sandwich fell in the water and a duck ate it!! 'OH NO!' I said, 'Eva, I'm SO hungry!'

Eva gave me one of her sandwiches because she is the best sister in the world! I was really happy and the duck was, too!

Later that day, when we were at the beach, I bought two big chocolate ice creams, one for Eva and one for me. YUM!

Fun boost

Draw and colour three favourite things in your YUMMY holiday sandwich.

Read the story. Draw what the children bought.

Zoe

Dan

Tom

Vicky

Peter

Eva

My birthday!

It was my tenth birthday last week. My friends and I went to a huge shopping centre with my parents. Then we went to a café and ate purple and green cupcakes! We had a great time because we all bought something we really like. Vicky bought a new skateboard, Dan bought a new book from the big bookshop and Eva bought a tennis racket because she plays every week. Tom got some new paints and Peter got a fantastic red guitar. Zoe bought a pair of roller skates. She loves them. The best thing was that my parents bought me some presents for my birthday! I got some orange ice skates and my favourite superhero comic books. What a GREAT day!

Fun boost

Choose three friends or family members. Today is their birthday! Write their names on each present!

Listening

Listen and draw lines. There is one extra person.

Emma   Jack   Lily   Paul

Charlie   Clare   Peter

Fun boost

Make a Mix-and-Match flip book.

1 Fold two sheets of A4 paper in half vertically.
2 Cut into three equal sections horizontally.
3 On each page, draw three foods, one in each section.
4 Mix and match the strips. Ask your family.

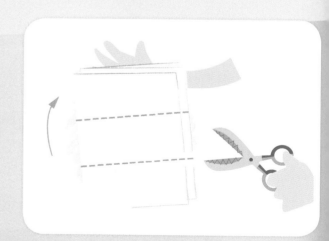

Do you like _____ with _____ and _____ ?

Listening

03 **Listen and number. Then complete the sentences.**

At the children's hospital

1 Ben has got a _____ and is thirsty.
2 Paul has got a cough and is very _____ .
3 Vicky has got an _____ .
4 Peter is weak and has got a _____ .
5 Zoe has got a very _____ toothache.

Fun boost

Choose an illness from the pictures. Mime and ask your family to say the illness.

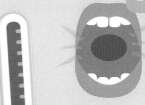

a cold

an earache

a cough

a toothache

tired

a stomach-ache

a temperature

Listening

04 **Aria is talking about things she wants to do this year. Listen and draw lines.**

1 big tree

2 ducks

3 ice cream

4 box of treasure

5 dolphins

6 rain

Aria

A a small house

B the sea

C a picnic

D the forest

E a shower

F chocolate ice cream

Fun boost

Think of six NEW exciting things you want to do next year. Write them here and show your family.

Listening

05 Listen to Omar and then play *That's not true!* with your family.

Example

Paul

Omar goes to Cairo on ___*Sundays*___ .

That's not true! He goes on ___*Fridays*___ !

Fred

1 He goes by plane.

That's not true! He goes by _____ .

2 On Friday afternoons, they go roller skating.

That's not true! They go _____ .

3 On Friday evenings, they play cards.

That's not true! They _____ _____ .

4 On Saturday mornings, they go shopping.

That's not true! They go _____ .

5 On Saturday afternoons, they go to the football stadium.

That's not true! They go to the _____ .

6 On Saturday evenings, they eat burgers.

That's not true! They eat _____ .

Fun boost

1 Days **2 Travel** **3 Sports** **4 Places** **5 Food**

A FUN weekend.
Choose one picture
(A, B or C) for
each group.
Tell your family
about your
weekend.

11

Listening

 06 **Listen and colour and write.**

Fun boost

Draw a CRAZY house with five CRAZY things around the house.

Are there any animals?

What people are there?

Where is your crazy house?

Writing

Look and spell the words.

These are my favourite places.

Jane

Example

sp o̲ r t s̲
c e̲ n t r e̲

l __ b r __ r __

__ a __ __ e t

f u __ f __ i __

s __ p __ r m __ r k __ t

__ i __ e __ a

Fun boost

Make a chart of your favourite places.

1 Draw a circle on a sheet of paper.

2 Divide the circle into six equal sections.

3 In each section, draw and colour a favourite place.

4 Show your chart to your family.

Writing

Sarah

Look at Sarah's favourite things. Write the words and the letters.

> photos   horse   pancakes   teddy bear   films   ~~plants~~   pasta

Example Sarah likes to water the ___plants___ every morning before school. [A]

1   She loves to watch funny _____ at the cinema with her family. ☐

2   She makes fantastic strawberry _____ for her sister's breakfast on Sundays. ☐

3   At bedtime, she sleeps with her favourite _____ _____ . ☐

4   She cooks yummy _____ with vegetables and cheese for her grandparents. ☐

5   She takes the best _____ on her phone at birthday parties! ☐

6   She enjoys _____ riding every Saturday morning. __

Fun boost

Find your favourite things and make a memory box.

1   Find a box with a lid.

2   Write your name on the box.

3   Put six of your favourite things (photos, small objects, etc.) in the box.

4   Hide it until you change schools!

My memory box

Writing

Complete the sentences.

Example My friends, Daisy, Jane, Fred and Jack, are _brilliant football players_ .

1 My cousin Charlie is the _____ _____ _____ in the world!

2 Last weekend, my best friend Vicky _____ _____ _____ .

3 My little brother Paul loves _____ _____ at school. He always wins!

4 Julia, Lily and I really _____ _____ at birthday parties.

5 My friends _____ _____ _____ .

6 _____ _____ _____ _____ _____ .

Fun boost

Can you do these things in your bedroom? Put a tick (✓) or a cross (✗). Then try them!

1 Throw and catch a ball. ☐
2 Kick or bounce a ball. ☐
3 Stand and hop on one leg. ☐
4 Swim on your bed. ☐
5 Dance to music. ☐
6 Jump up and down on the bed. ☐

Writing

Read and write the correct words on the lines.

horse   jump   dolphin   Wednesday   dream   ~~friends~~

Karim's blog

Karim

My pet sheep

My pet sheep is called Peter. He is VERY, VERY funny and makes my family, *friends* and me laugh a lot. He loves to **1** _____ and sometimes thinks he is another animal!

On Monday, he wanted to be a **2** _____ and my cousin took him riding. On Tuesday, he wanted to be a kangaroo and my family watched him **3** _____ up in the sky. He was fantastic!

On **4** _____ , he wanted to be a monkey. I played some music and Peter did lots of fun dances around our farm. It was brilliant!

On Thursday, he wanted to run in a race and on Friday, he wanted to be a **5** _____ and he entered a swimming competition. He jumped in the lake and was really good. We were all very surprised. He is the best pet in the world!

Fun boost

Choose an imaginary pet. Draw your pet and four things it wants to do.

Writing

Read Daisy's and Jim's adventure stories.
Write the best titles on the lines.

Story 1 _____

Yesterday, I went to the jungle and saw an elephant who said, 'I'm hungry!' I answered, 'Don't eat me!' The elephant said, 'I don't eat children, only cheese and chocolate sandwiches!'

A My favourite lunch

B My jungle adventure

C I don't like cheese

Daisy

A My trip to the circus

B I'm a great skater

C The day I flew up a mountain!

Story 2 _____

I love to dress up and roller skate. One afternoon, an alien asked, 'Can you skate up the mountain?' I answered, 'Fly me up!' So he did. It was snowing at the top!

Jim

Fun boost

Make an eight-page mini book to tell an adventure story.

1 Fold a sheet of paper in half.

2 Fold it in half again.

3 Use scissors to cut along the two top folded edges to the centre.

4 Draw pictures about your adventure story and write sentences.

5 Add a title to the front of your book and show it to your family.

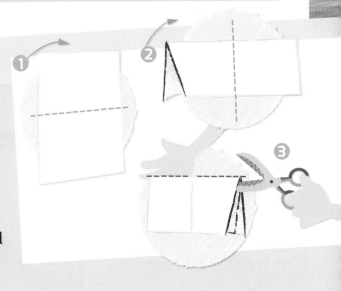

Writing

Look and complete the sentences. Use your own words.

Example Lily is with her _best friends_ .

1　They are eating cheese and tomato _____ .

2　Fred is having a family _____ with his mum, dad and _____ .

3　They are sitting on the _____ in a huge _____ .

4　Paul is at the _____ with his _____ .

5　He is eating his favourite _____ .

6　Daisy is with her _____ and they are having _____ .

7　There are lots of yummy things to _____ .

Fun boost

Draw two drinks in the picnic baskets and six foods on the blanket.
Ask your family or friends to come to the picnic!

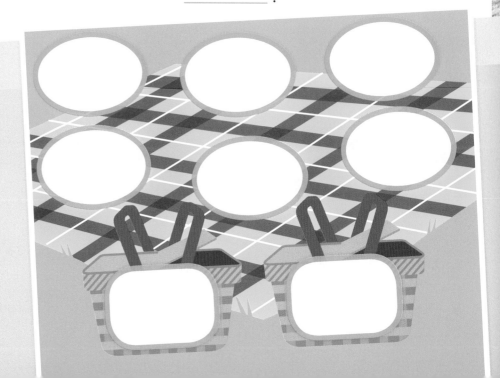

18

Writing

Look at Lucy's photos of her friends and write sentences.

Example Daisy *is sailing on the lake.*

1 Josh _____

2 Alex _____

3 Sam _____

Fun boost

Choose two friends.
Take a photo or
draw them.
Tell your family
about your friends.

19

Speaking

Grace and her mum love pizza! Look and circle four differences.

Grace is eating the pizza with her hands, but her mum is ...

Fun boost

Draw four CRAZY things on the pizzas and write FUN pizza names. Tell your family what is different.

My pizza name is

_____ .

My family's pizza name is

_____ .

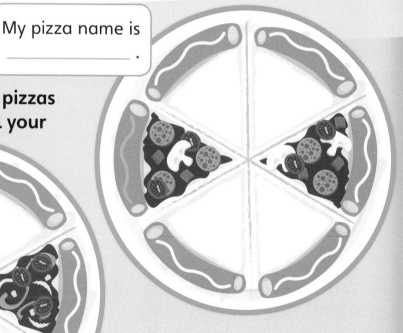

My pizza has got strawberries and ice cream, but my family's has got pasta and meatballs!

Speaking

Look at Amy's crazy weather day yesterday. What was the weather like? What did she do? Tell your family.

AMY'S DAY
morning
lunchtime
afternoon
evening

Fun boost

Draw four weather icons and four FUN activities. Tell your family about your day!

morning

lunchtime

afternoon

evening

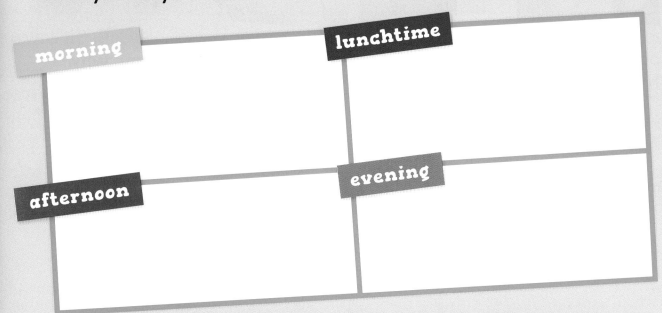

Yesterday morning, it snowed and I went swimming in the sea with my friends.

Speaking

The milkshake is different. The sandwich, salad and burger are food, you eat them. You don't eat a milkshake – you drink it!

Example

1

2

3

4

Look at the pictures. Tell your family which one is different and why. There is one example.

Fun boost

Draw four pictures. Ask your family which one is different and why.

22

Speaking

1 **Read Sam's questions and Jack's answers about school.**

Sam

Jack

Who do you play with at school?

I play with an alien!

What games do you play at school?

I play hockey and go skateboarding.

What do you have for school lunch?

I have mango milkshake and rice with vegetables.

The first one is false!

Yes!

2 **Now choose FRIENDS or HOBBIES. Answer the questions. Say two true answers and one false answer. Can your family guess which is false?**

Friends

1 Who is your best friend?
2 How often do you visit your friends?
3 Where do you go with your friends after school?

Hobbies

1 What is your favourite hobby?
2 Where do you do your hobby?
3 Who do you do your hobby with?

Fun boost

Ask and answer with your family.

1 Pretend to be someone famous from TV like a singer or a dancer or an actor.
2 Your family can ask SIX questions to guess who you are. For example, *How old are you? Where do you live? What do you like?*
3 Then swap: someone in your family pretends to be someone famous.

Speaking

1 **Read about the boy's dream.**

> I had a dream last night and I was in a comic-book story with a lion. We went on a picnic and we wore helmets!

2 **Tell your family about your last dream. It can be a real or imaginary dream.**

1 What did you do in your dream?
2 Where did you go?
3 Who were you with?
4 Was it exciting? Why? / Why not?

Fun boost

**Make a paper-plate dream catcher.
Ask your family for help.**

1 Cut out the centre of the paper plate.
2 Decorate the ring and make some holes.
3 Cut a long string and put it through the holes in different directions.
4 Cut four strings and tie a feather on them. Add some beads!
5 Make a loop and hang up your dream catcher!

Skippy – the coolest dancer!

07 Skippy loves music and is a FANTASTIC dancer.

At school, he wears roller skates and dances in the classroom and the playground.

His dancing sometimes makes our teacher angry, but when the music plays, Skippy jumps and bounces around.

We video his dances on our phones and clap very loudly!
He is really COOOOOOOL!

**Choose two COOL dance moves.
Draw Skippy doing your two
dance moves.**

Oksi's parrot is 100!

08 Oksi has a purple pet parrot called Sally.

Yesterday was Sally's 100th birthday and Oksi gave her a HUGE party! Sally's friends came to the party and they all wore purple clothes.

They sang *Happy Birthday* and gave Sally lots of presents and a very big cake with 100 candles!

Sally is very lucky to have friends to help her have a special birthday.

Happy 100th

Choose three presents for Sally's birthday. Draw your presents here.

Milo's fun weekend hobby!

09 Milo dresses up in lots of different funny clothes at the weekends.

After school on Fridays, she dresses as a clown and makes people laugh at the circus!

On Saturdays, she dresses as a pirate and goes sailing with her pet parrot!

On Sundays, she dresses as a pop star and sings her favourite songs!

Choose and dress up as a fun job. Take a photo or draw a picture here.

Pixy is super sporty!

10 My friend Pixy is SUPER sporty. Think of any sport ...

Pixy is brilliant at it!

He is always first in games at the sports centre. He plays tennis and football very well.

He is a great swimmer and the best skateboarder in the class.

BUT he is not good at doing English homework and is sometimes naughty in the swimming pool. He hides under the water!

Write what you are good at here.

I'm the best at ...

I'm great at ...

I'm brilliant at ...

Brave Bolt is never afraid!

11 Bolt went on a trip to the dangerous forest last week.

When a huge bear came, Bolt ran quickly.

When a terrible crocodile came, Bolt swam quietly.

When a loud lion came, Bolt shouted, 'I'm not frightened!'

When a scary spider came, Bolt hid behind a tall tree.

Bolt is clever and really brave!

Be Bolt, the bear, the crocodile, the lion and the spider! Act it out with your friends or family.

GRRR!

Woody the brilliant bookworm!

12 Woody LOVES to read a different English book every day.

She has hundreds of easy and difficult books on her bookcase. Sometimes, she reads e-books on websites.

Her favourites are storybooks – sad stories, funny stories, scary stories, travel stories, adventure stories … ANY stories!

Because she loves reading morning, afternoon and evening, and at the breakfast table …

... on the bus and in the bath,
we call her a 'bookworm'.

A bookworm

Write fun names for the two books on the covers.

Cambridge University Press
www.cambridge.org/elt

Cambridge Assessment English
www.cambridgeenglish.org

Information on this title:
www.cambridge.org/9781108563673

© Cambridge University Press and Cambridge Assessment 2020

This publication is in copyright. Subject to statutory exception and to the provisions of relevant collective licensing agreements, no reproduction of any part may take place without the written permission of Cambridge University Press.

First published 2020

20 19 18 17 16 15 14 13 12 11 10 9 8

Printed in Poland by Opolgraf

A catalogue record for this publication is available from the British Library

ISBN 978-1-108-56367-3 Student's Book and Home
                          Booklet with Online Activities

The publishers have no responsibility for the persistence or accuracy of URLs for external or third-party internet websites referred to in this publication, and do not guarantee that any content on such websites is, or will remain, accurate or appropriate. Information regarding prices, travel timetables, and other factual information given in this work is correct at the time of first printing but the publishers do not guarantee the accuracy of such information thereafter.

Author acknowledgements

The author would like to sincerely thank Audrey Cowan for her encouraging editorial style and Felicity Harwood for being a great sounding board during the ideas generation process.

Publisher acknowledgements

The authors and publishers are grateful to Robert Hill for reviewing the content and style of the stories.

Acknowledgements

The authors and publishers acknowledge the following sources of copyright material and are grateful for the permissions granted. While every effort has been made, it has not always been possible to identify the sources of all the material used, or to trace all copyright holders. If any omissions are brought to our notice, we will be happy to include the appropriate acknowledgements on reprinting and in the next update to the digital edition, as applicable.

Key: BG = Background

Photography

BG: Pete Lomchid/Moment; Jay's photo/Moment; Sergi Escribano/Moment; Alina Siamionava/EyeEm; Marka/Universal Images Group; **Reading:** Cherry Tantirathanon/EyeEm; robas/E+; komyvgory/iStock/Getty Images Plus; Emilija Manevska/Moment; Slawomir Tomas/EyeEm; Punnawit Suwuttananun/Moment; DAJ; 2A Images; Per Eriksson; Ramn Carretero/EyeEm; **Listening:** Maskot; Westend61; Erick Olvera/EyeEm; Indeed; Thiti Sukapan/EyeEm; hadynyah/E+; Emma Kim/Cultura; Massimo Lama/EyeEm; hdere/E+; jreika/iStock/Getty Images Plus; by Martin Deja/Moment; krisanapong detraphiphat/Moment; GMVozd/E+; BananaStock; kwanchaichaiudom/iStock/Getty Images Plus; 1MoreCreative/iStock/Getty Images Plus; Ismailciydem/iStock/Getty Images Plus; Sawitree Pamee/EyeEm; Christophe Bourloton/iStock/Getty Images Plus; Jasmin Merdan/Moment; Esther Moreno Martinez/EyeEm; **Writing:** Compassionate Eye Foundation/Natasha Alipour Faridani/DigitalVision; Hufton and Crow/Corbis Documentary; Dave Shafer/Aurora; Stephen Dorey/Photolibrary; Nikada/iStock Unreleased; Tom Sibley/Corbis; AFP; Morsa Images/DigitalVision; Giovanna Graf/EyeEm; Gerard Puigmal/Moment; Louis Turner/Cultura; Bob Peterson/UpperCut Images; jreika/iStock/Getty Images Plus; Aliraza Khatri's Photography/Moment; amenic181/iStock/Getty Images Plus; Steve Debenport/E+; Shoji Fujita/DigitalVision; Jose Luis Pelaez Inc/DigitalVision; Jupiterimages/Polka Dot/Getty Images Plus; Ty Allison/Taxi; Mark Hunt; Seb Oliver/Cultura; Tony Garcia/Image Source; LifeJourneys/E+; photography by Linda Lyon/Moment; Matthew Ashmore/EyeEm; MARK HICKEN/Alamy Stock Photo; Eakachai Leesin/EyeEm; Westend61; Nancy Honey/Cultura; Andersen Ross/Stockbyte; Monkey Business Images; Chiyacat/iStock/Getty Images Plus; PeopleImages/E+; Artyom Geodakyan/TASS; Godong/Universal Images Group; Esther Moreno Martinez/EyeEm; Emma Kim/Cultura; **Speaking:** EujarimPhotography/Moment; PeopleImages/E+; RichVintage/E+; photosindia; **Brave Bolt is never afraid!:** Barrett Hedges/National Geographic Image Collection; Krzysztof Dydynski/Lonely Planet Images/Getty Images Plussss; Don Baird/Moment; Images from BarbAnna/Moment.

The following photograph is sourced from other library.

Writing: MARK HICKEN/Alamy Stock Photo.

Front cover photography and illustrations by Amanda Enright; Jhonny Nunez; Leo Trinidad; Pol Cunyat; Dan Widdowson; Pipi Sposito; P and P Studio/Shutterstock; Piotr Urakau/Shutterstock.

Illustrations

Leo Trinidad (Bright); Amanda Enright (Advocate); Fran and David Brylewska (Beehive); Dave Williams (Bright); Pablo Gallego (Beehive); Pipi Sposito (Advocate); Collaborate Agency; Wild Apple Design.

Audio

Audio Production by DN and AE Strauss Ltd, with engineer Mike Dentith and by Ian Harker.

Design

Design and typeset by Wild Apple Design Ltd
Cover design by Collaborate agency.